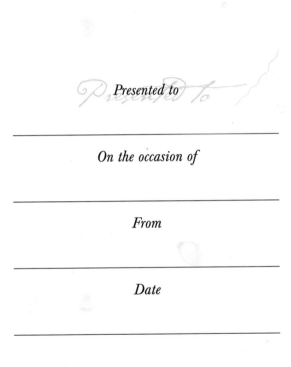

Presented to

_____

On the occasion of

_____

From

_____

Date

_____

SELECTIONS FROM
STEPPING HEAVENWARD

ELIZABETH PRENTISS

BARBOUR
PUBLISHING, INC.

© 2000 by Barbour Publishing, Inc.

ISBN 1-57748-717-6

All Scripture quotations are taken from the King James Version of the Bible.

Published by Barbour Publishing, Inc., P. O. Box 719, Uhrichsville, Ohio 44683
www.barbourbooks.com

 Member of the
Evangelical Christian
Publishers Association

Printed in China.

Table of Contents

Introduction

Elizabeth Prentiss wrote *Stepping Heavenward* more than a hundred years ago—and yet her voice is still sharp and clear, full of spiritual insight and practical wisdom. What makes the story so freshly unique is the transparency and genuineness of Katy, the heroine. She is no saintly, romantic figure, but a flesh-and-blood woman whose faults we recognize as our own. The novel records her life's journey, from self-centered adolescence to spiritual maturity. We see ourselves in Katy, for we, too, have lived the same everyday trials she experiences.

Mrs. Prentiss stressed that Christ calls us each to a life of total consecration. That life of complete surrender, however, is lived out in ordinary, even trivial ways. Moment by moment, we walk with God, giving Him more and more of our hearts, until the day when we reach our journey's end.

As you read this selection of thoughts from Mrs. Prentiss's novel, may you, too, be inspired to "step heavenward."

The Beginning of the Road: God's Love for Me

*"For God so loved the world,
that he gave his only begotten Son,
that whosoever believeth in him should not perish,
but have everlasting life."*

JOHN 3:16

When Katy is discouraged, full of confusion and frustration, her pastor, Dr. Cabot, helps her to comprehend Christ's love. . .

"I am very glad to see you, my dear child," said Dr. Cabot.

I intended to be very dignified and cold. . . . But those few kind words just upset me, and I began to cry.

"You wouldn't speak to me so kindly," I got out at last, "if you knew what a dreadful creature I am. I am angry with myself and angry with everybody and angry with God. I can't be good two minutes at a time. I do everything I do not want to do and do nothing I try and pray to do. Everybody plagues me and tempts me. And God does not answer any of my prayers, and I am just desperate."

"Poor child!" he said in a low voice, as if to himself. "Poor, heartsick, tired child that cannot see what I can see, that her Father's loving arms are all about her!"

Nay, in all these things we are more than conquerors through him that loved us.
ROMANS 8:37

"I am a wayward, foolish child. But He loves me! I have disobeyed and grieved Him ten thousand times. But He loves me! I have lost faith in some of my dearest friends and am very desolate. But He loves me! I do not love Him; I am even angry with Him! But He loves me!"

I knelt down to pray, and all my wasted, childish,
wicked life came and stared me in the face. I looked at it
and said with tears of joy, "But He loves me!"
Never in my life did I feel so rested, so quieted, so sorrowful,
and yet so satisfied.

*You are one of the Lord's beloved ones,
though perhaps you do not know it.*

Nor height, nor depth, nor any other creature,
shall be able to separate us from the love of God,
which is in Christ Jesus our Lord.
Romans 8:39

All this time, while I was caring
for nobody but myself
and fancying He must almost hate me,
He was loving and pitying me.

"As the Father hath loved me, so have I loved you:
continue ye in my love."
John 15:9

God's children please Him just as well when they sit patiently with folded hands, if that is His will, as when they are hard at work.

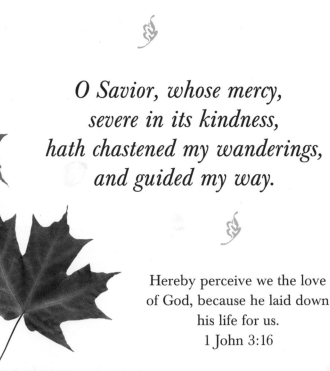

O Savior, whose mercy,
severe in its kindness,
hath chastened my wanderings,
and guided my way.

Hereby perceive we the love of God, because he laid down his life for us.
1 John 3:16

I have been sick, and I know what sorrow means. . . .
And I am glad that I do. For I have learned Christ in that school,
and I know He can comfort when no one else can.

If we abuse His gifts by letting them take His place in our hearts,
it is an act of love on His part to take them away
or to destroy our pleasure in them.

A sufferer he certainly is who sees a great and good
and terrible God who cannot look upon iniquity
and does not see His risen Son,
who lives to intercede for us before the throne of the Father.

The Beginning of the Road

There is no wilderness so dreary but that His love can illuminate it;
no desolation so desolate but that He can sweeten it.
I know what I am saying. It is no delusion.

*Herein is love, not that we loved God,
but that he loved us,
and sent his Son to be the propitiation
for our sins.*
1 JOHN 4:10

The LORD thy God in the midst of thee. . .will rejoice over thee with joy;
he will rest in his love, he will joy over thee with singing.
Zephaniah 3:17

A Long, Slow Journey:
Applying God's Grace to Our Sin

A Long, Slow Journey

*O*nce my heart responds to God's love, I quickly become discouraged by my own sinful nature. In moments of emotion, I promise myself that I will certainly fly straight to heaven—but all too soon, I return to the ordinary difficulties of daily life. I am disappointed to find that I am just as selfish and easily irritated, just as full of pride and impatience as ever. My progress toward heaven goes in fits and spurts.

But these fluctuations in the spiritual life are normal. I cannot make myself holy, any more than I could give myself eternal life. Both those things are Christ's job—and as I give myself to Christ moment by moment, day after day, His redeeming power continues to work in my life, making me whole.

For that which I do I allow not: for what I would, that do I not; but what I hate, that do I.

God's divine nature will supplant our human nature
if we only consent to let Him work in us of
His own good pleasure.

*Our course heavenward is like the plan
of the zealous pilgrim of old, who
for every three steps forward,
took one backward.*

How easy it is to make good resolutions,
and how easy it is to break them!

For I know that in me (that is, in my flesh,) dwelleth no good thing: for to will is present with me; but how to perform that which is good I find not. For the good that I would I do not: but the evil which I would not, that I do.

Romans 7:18–19

*I wish I knew
whether anybody exactly
as bad as I am
ever got to heaven
at last?*

Katy is surprised to learn that her mother once struggled with the same faults she does. . .

"Dear child," she said, "how I pity that you have inherited my quick, irritable temper."

"Yours, Mother!" I cried out. "What can you mean?"

Mother smiled a little at my surprise. "It is even so," she said.

"Then how did you cure yourself of it? Tell me quick, Mother, and let me cure myself of mine."

"My dear Katy," she said, "I wish I could make you see that God is just as willing and just as able to sanctify as He is to redeem us. It would save you so much weary, disappointing work. But God has opened my eyes at last."

"I wish He would open mine, then," I said, "for all I see now is that I am just as horrid as I can be and that the more I pray the worse I grow."

"That is not true, dear," she replied. "Go on praying—pray without ceasing."

A Long, Slow Journey

It is high time to stop and think. I have been like one running a race and am stopping to take a breath. I see that if I would be happy in God, I must give Him all. And there is a wicked reluctance to do that. I want Him—but I want to have my own way, too. I want to walk humbly and softly before Him, and I want to go where I shall be admired and applauded. To whom shall I yield? To God? Or to myself?

Today I feel discouraged and disappointed. I certainly thought that if God really loved me and I really loved Him, I should find myself growing better day by day. But I am not improved in the least. Most of the time I spend on my knees I am either stupid, feeling nothing at all, or else my head is full of what I was doing before I began to pray or what I am going to do as soon as I get through. I do not believe anybody else in the world is like me in this respect. Then when I feel differently and can make a nice, glib prayer, with floods of tears running down my cheeks, I get all puffed up and think how pleased God must be to see me so fervent in spirit. I go downstairs in this frame and begin to complain to our maid, Susan, for misplacing my music, till all of a sudden I catch myself doing it and stop short, crestfallen and confounded. I have so many such experiences that I feel like a baby just learning to walk, who is so afraid of falling that it has half a mind to sit down once and for all.

Now if I do that I would not, it is no more I that do it, but sin that dwelleth in me.
ROMANS 7:20

*O wretched man that I am! who shall deliver me
from the body of this death?
I thank God through Jesus Christ our Lord.
So then with the mind I myself serve the law
of God; but with the flesh the law of sin.*
ROMANS 7:24–25

*hen Katy confesses her spiritual problems to her pastor's wife, she is surprised
when instead of being shocked, Mrs. Cabot bursts into laughter.*

"Do excuse me for laughing at you, you dear child, you!" she said. "But I remember so well how I used to flounder through such needless anxieties; and life looks so different, so very different, to me now from what it did then! What should you think of a man, who having just sowed his field, was astonished not to see it at once ripe for the harvest because his neighbor's, after long months of waiting, was just being gathered in?"

You must make the most of what little Christian life you have;
be thankful God has given you so much, cherish it, pray over it,
and guard it like the apple of your eye. Imperceptibly, but surely,
it will grow and keep on growing, for this is its nature.

The righteous shall flourish like the palm tree:
he shall grow like a cedar in Lebanon.
PSALM 92:12

He never leaves His work incomplete, and He will gradually lead you
into clear and open vision if you will allow Him to do it.
I say gradually, because I believe this to be His usual method,
while I do not deny that there are cases
where light suddenly bursts in like a flood.

A Long, Slow Journey

*M*ake your complaint, tell Him how obscure everything still looks to you, and beg Him to complete your cure. He may see fit to try your faith and patience by delaying this completion; but meanwhile you are safe in His presence, and while led by His hand, He will excuse the mistakes you make and pity your falls. But you will imagine that it is best that He should enable you at once to see clearly. If it is, you may be sure He will do it. He never makes mistakes. But He often deals far differently with His disciples. He lets them grope their way in the dark until they fully learn how blind they are, how helpless, how absolutely in need of Him.

Knowing this, that our old man is crucified with him, that the body of sin might be destroyed, that henceforth we should not serve sin.
ROMANS 6:6

*P*rayer is the way I open my heart to God. If I live my life in a constant state of prayer, as the apostle Paul tells me I should, then the line between God's heart and mine will always be open. Then love will flow into my life and out to others, for prayer connects me to Jesus.

Pray without ceasing.
1 THESSALONIANS 5:17

Dear Mother! She has gone now,
where she always goes when she feels sad, straight to God.

It is hard work to pray. It tires me. And I do wish there was some easy way of growing good. In fact, I should like to have God send a sweet temper to me just as He sent bread and meat to Elijah.

But Mother says, "I do wish I could make you love to pray, my darling child. If you only knew the strength, and the light, and the joy you might have for the simple asking. God attaches no conditions to His gifts. He only says, 'Ask!' "

I would pray about my little finger if my little finger went astray.

"And all things, whatsoever ye shall ask in prayer,
believing, ye shall receive."
Matthew 21:22

Strength for the Way

Only through prayer can I learn who Christ really is. . .

"Have you a perfectly distinct, settled view of what Christ is to the human soul?"

"I do not know. I understand, of course, more or less perfectly, that my salvation depends on Him alone; it is His gift."

"But do you see with equal clearness that your sanctification must be as fully His gift as your salvation is?"

"No," I said after a little thought. "I have had the feeling that He has done His part and now I must do mine."

"My dear, then the first thing you have to do is learn Christ."

"But how?"

"On your knees, my child, on your knees."

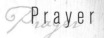

Every prayer offered in the name of Jesus is sure to have its answer. Every such prayer is dictated by the Holy Spirit and therefore finds acceptance with God; and if your cry did not prevail with Him as we may hope it did, then He has answered it in some other way.

Continue in prayer,
and watch in the same with thanksgiving.
COLOSSIANS 4:2

Likewise the Spirit also helpeth our infirmities: for we know not what we should pray for as we ought: but the Spirit itself maketh intercession for us with groanings which cannot be uttered.
Romans 8:26

Strength for the Way

I have learned, at least, to face and fight distractions
instead of running away from them as I used to do.
My faith in prayer and resort to it become more and more
the foundation of my life. Nothing but prayer
stands between my soul and the best gifts of God;
in other words, that I can and shall get what I ask for.

I sometimes find it a help, when dull and cramped
in my devotions, to say to myself:
"Suppose Christ should now appear before you,
and you could see Him as He appeared to His disciples on earth,
what would you say to Him?"
This brings Him near, and I say what I would say
if He were visibly present.

ike Katy, we can benefit from these thoughts on prayer written by a seven-teenth-century man named Fenelon:

QUESTION: In my prayers my mind has difficulty in finding anything to say to God. My heart is not in it, or it is inaccessible to the thoughts of my mind.

REPLY: It is not necessary to say much to God. Oftentimes one does not speak much to a friend whom one is delighted to see; one looks at him with pleasure; one speaks certain short words to him that are mere expressions of feeling. The mind has no part in them, or next to none; one keeps repeating the same words. It is not so much a variety of thoughts that one seeks in intercourse with a friend as a certain repose and correspondence of heart. It is thus we are with God. A word, a sigh, a sentiment says it all to God; it is not always necessary to have transports. Content one's self with giving to Him what He gives it to give. And even while receiving emotional gifts, prepare yourself by pure faith for the time when you might be deprived of them.

I cannot make myself holy; only Christ can do that. But I can choose to exercise my will for God. Just as a married couple commits themselves to each other, I commit myself to Christ. This is an active decision, one that affects the way I live my entire life. Like marriage, however, it is not a decision that can be made once and then be done with it; instead, I must choose to commit myself to God's will daily.

Teach me to do thy will;
for thou art my God:
thy spirit is good;
lead me into the land of uprightness.
Psalm 143:10

Traveling Further

Traveling

n older saint, Mrs. Campbell, gives Katy spiritual advice about accepting God's will:

"You know," I began, "dear Mrs. Campbell, that there are some trials that cannot do us any good. They only call out all there is in us that is unlovely and severe."

"I don't know of any such trials," she replied.

"Suppose you had to live with people who were perfectly uncongenial, who misunderstood you, and who were always getting into your way as stumbling blocks?"

"If I were living with them and they made me unhappy, I would ask God to relieve me of this trial if He thought it best. If He did not think it best, I would then try to find out the reason. He might have two reasons. One would be the good they might do me. The other, the good I might do them."

"But in the case I was supposing, neither party can be of the least use to the other."

"You forget perhaps the indirect good one may gain by living with uncongenial, tempting persons. First, such people do good by the very self-denial and self-control their mere presence demands. Then, their making one's home less homelike and perfect than it would be in their absence may help to render our real home in heaven more attractive."

"But suppose one cannot exercise self-control and is always flying out and flaring up?" I objected.

"I should say that a Christian who was always doing that," she replied gravely, "was in pressing need of just the trial God sent when He shut that person up to such a life of hourly temptation. We only know ourselves and what we really are when the force of circumstances bring us out."

"For whosoever shall do
the will of God,
the same
is my brother,
and my sister,
and mother."
MARK 3:35

Traveling Further

*I*t has been said "that a fixed, inflexible will is a great assistance in a holy life."

* You can will to read books that will stimulate you in your Christian life rather than those that merely amuse.

* You can will to use every means of grace appointed by God.

* You can will to spend much time in prayer without regard to your frame at the moment.

* You can will to prefer a religion of principle to one of mere feeling; in other words, to obey the will of God when no comfortable glow of emotion accompanies your obedience.

You cannot will to possess the spirit of Christ; that must come as His gift; but you can choose to study His life and to imitate it.

fter moments spent on the spiritual mountaintops, coming down to earth can be a rude awakening. . .

The very gates of heaven seemed open to let me in. And then they were suddenly shut in my face, and I found myself a poor, weak, tempted creature here upon the earth. I, who fancied myself an heir of glory, was nothing but a peevish, human creature—very human indeed. . .in short, my own poor faulty self once more. Oh, what fearful battles I fought for patience, forbearance, and unselfishness! What sorrowful tears of shame I shed over hasty, impatient words and fretful tones! No wonder I longed to be gone where weakness should be swallowed up in strength and sin give place to eternal perfection!

But here I am, and suffering and work lie before me, for which I feel little physical or mental courage. But "blessed be the will of God."

To be at work, to be useful, to be necessary to my husband and children is just what I want; and I find it hard to be set against the wall, as it were, like an old piece of furniture no longer of any service.

I see now that my first desire has not been to please God but to please myself, for I am restless under His restraining hand.

"Thy kingdom come. Thy will be done in earth, as it is in heaven."

MATTHEW 6:10

It is easy, in theory, to let God plan our destiny and that of our friends. But when it comes to a specific case, we fancy we can help His judgment with our poor reason. Well, I must go to Him with this new anxiety.

*O*nce again Katy seeks for wisdom on trials from her older friend, Mrs. Campbell:

"Doesn't it seem hard, when you think of the many happy homes there are in the world, that you should be singled out for such bereavement and loneliness?"

She replied with a smile: "I am not singled out, dear. There are thousands of God's own children scattered over the world suffering far more than I do. And I do not think there are many persons who are happier than I am. I was bound to my God and Savior before I knew a sorrow, it is true. But it was by a chain of many links; and every link that dropped away brought me to Him till at last, having nothing left, I was shut up to Him and learned fully what I had only learned partially, how soul-satisfying He is."

*It is feeling sorry for ourselves
that dishonors God, not grief.*

God's ways are infinitely perfect; we are to love Him
for what He is and therefore equally as much when
He afflicts as when He prospers us; there is no real happiness
but in doing and suffering His will; and this life is
but a scene of probation through
which we pass to the real life above.

Consenting to suffer does not annul the suffering.

Bishop Wilson charges us to bear all things "as unto God" and
"with the greatest privacy." How seldom I have met difficulties
save as lions in my way that I would avoid if I could,
and how I have tormented my friends
by tedious complaints about them!

How can I fret
at anything which
is the will of God?
Let Him take all beside;
He has given me Himself.
I love,
I praise Him
every moment.

I think I may say of my happiness that it rests on something higher
and deeper than even my husband and children: The will of God,
the sweet will of God. If He should take them all away,
I might still possess a peace which would flow on forever.

Traveling Further

I am constantly forgetting to recognize God's hand in the little, everyday trials of life, and instead of receiving them as from Him, find fault with the instruments by which He sends them. I can give up my child, my only brother, my darling mother without a word; but to receive every tiresome visitor as sent expressly and directly to weary me by the Master Himself; to meet every negligence on the part of the servants as His choice for me at the moment; to be satisfied and patient when my husband gets particularly absorbed in his books, because my Father sees that little discipline suitable for me at the time; all this I have not fully learned.

Casting down imaginations, and every high thing
that exalteth itself against the knowledge of God,
and bringing into captivity
every thought to the obedience of Christ.

2 CORINTHIANS 10:5

It is a religion of principle—setting our wills on doing what is right—that
God wants from us, not one of mere feeling.

*B*ring into captivity every thought to the obedience of Christ.
Take what I cannot give—my heart, body, thoughts, time, abilities,
money, health, strength, nights, days, youth, age—and spend them in Thy
service, O my crucified Master, Redeemer, God. Oh, let these not be
mere words! Whom have I in heaven but Thee? And there is no one
upon earth that I desire in comparison to Thee. My heart is athirst
for God, the living God.

You may not understand why He leads you now in this way
and now in that, but you may, nay, you must believe
that perfection is stamped on His every act.

*I*f you find, in the course of daily events, that your self-consecration is not perfect—that is, that your will revolts at His will—do not be discouraged, but fly to your Savior and stay in His presence till you obtain the spirit in which He cried in His hour of anguish, "Father, if thou be willing, remove this cup from me: nevertheless not my will, but thine, be done" (Luke 22:42). Every time you do this it will be easier to do it; every such consent to suffer will bring you nearer and nearer to Him, and in this nearness to Him you will find such peace, such blessed, sweet peace as will make your life infinitely happy, no matter what may be its mere outside conditions.

I delight to do thy will, O my God:
yea, thy law is within my heart.
PSALM 40:8

If I love God I will give myself completely to Him, surrendering each person and thing in my life to His care. I do not need to be afraid to do this, though, as I would if God were a human being asking me to make this sort of surrender. God not only asks me to give everything to Him, but He has already given everything to me, including His own Son; His love and commitment to me are far greater than I can ever imagine. Loving Him requires me to totally abandon myself–but my life is completely safe in His hands.

And walk in love,
as Christ also hath loved us,
and hath given himself for us.
EPHESIANS 5:2

I have a great deal to learn. I am like a child who cannot run to get what he wants but approaches it step by step, slowly, timidly—and yet approaches it. I am amazed at the patience of my blessed Master and Teacher, but how I love His school!

You cannot prove to yourself that you love God by examining your feelings toward Him. They are indefinite and they fluctuate. But just as far as you obey Him, just so far, depend upon it, you love Him. It is not natural to us sinful, ungrateful human beings to prefer His pleasure to our own or to follow His way instead of our own way, and nothing, nothing but love of Him can or does make us obedient to Him.

"If ye keep my commandments, ye shall abide in my love;
even as I have kept my Father's commandments, and abide in his love."
John 15:10

You might obey your mother from fear, but only for a season.
If you had no real love for her, you would gradually cease
to dread her displeasure; whereas it is the very nature
of love to grow stronger and more
influential every hour.

Do everything you do for Him
who has loved you
and given Himself for you.

It has seemed to me for several days that it must be that I really do love
God, though ever so little. But it shot through my mind today like a knife
that it is a miserable, selfish love at best, not worth my giving, not worth
God's accepting. All my old misery has come back with seven other

miseries more miserable than itself.

When I told Dr. Cabot, he could not help smiling as he said:

"When I see a little infant caressing its mother, would you have me say to it, 'You selfish child, how dare you pretend to caress your mother in that way? You are quite unable to appreciate her character; you love her merely because she loves you, treats you kindly'?"

It was my turn now to smile at my own folly.

"You are as yet but a babe in Christ," Dr. Cabot continued. "You love your God and Savior because He first loved you. The time will come when the character of your love will become changed into one which sees and feels the beauty and the perfection of its object."

*H*e has bought you with a price, and you are no longer your own. "But," you may reply, "this is contrary to my nature. I love my own way. I desire ease and pleasure; I desire to go to heaven, but I want to be carried thither on a bed of flowers. Can I not give myself so far to God as to feel a sweet sense of peace with Him, and be sure of final salvation, and yet, to a certain extent, indulge and gratify myself? If I give myself entirely away to Him and lose all ownership in myself, He may deny me many things I greatly desire. He may make my life hard and wearisome, depriving me of all that now makes it agreeable." But, I reply, this is no matter of parley and discussion; it is not optional with God's children whether they will pay Him a part of the price they owe Him and keep back the rest. He asks, and He has a right to ask, for all you have and all you are. And if you shrink from what is involved in such a surrender, you should fly to Him at once and never rest till He has conquered this secret disinclination to give to Him as freely and as fully as He has given to you. It is true that such an act of consecration on your part may involve a great deal of future discipline and correction. But as soon as you become the Lord's by your own deliberate and conscious act, He will begin that process of sanctification which is to make you holy as He is holy, perfect as He is perfect. He becomes at once your Physician as well as your dearest and best Friend, but He will use no painful remedy that can be avoided.

But the fruit of the Spirit is love, joy, peace,
longsuffering, gentleness, goodness, faith. . .
GALATIANS 5:22

Having been pardoned by your God and Savior, the next thing you have
to do is to show your gratitude for this infinite favor by consecrating your
self entirely to Him, body, soul, and spirit. This is the least you can do.

In reading the Bible I advise you to choose detached passages,
or even one verse a day, rather than a whole chapter.
Study every word;
ponder and pray over it
till you have got from it all the truth it contains.

51

Some liberty of action He must leave us or we should become mere machines. I think that those who love Him and wait upon Him day by day learn His will almost imperceptibly and need not go astray.

That Christ may dwell in your hearts by faith; that ye, being rooted and grounded in love. . .
EPHESIANS 3:17

The Christian life is a hidden life, known only by the eye that seeth in secret.

The question is not whether you ever gave yourself to God,
but whether you are His now.

Don't look back to the past; it is useless. Give yourself to Christ now.

And we have known and believed the love that God hath to us. God is
love; and he that dwelleth in love dwelleth in God, and God in him.
1 John 4:16

God means us to be always ascending, always getting nearer to Himself,
always learning something new about Him, always loving Him
better and better.

Walking with God

He reveals Himself to us in so many sorrows and so many joys.

Yes, I love everybody! That crowning joy has come to me at last. Christ is in my soul; He is mine; I am as conscious of it as that my husband and children are mine; and His Spirit flows forth from mine in the calm peace of a river whose banks are green with grass and glad with flowers.

We love him,
because he first loved us.
1 JOHN 4:19

My Fellow Travelers:
Living with Others in Love and Peace

If I am not more and more controlled
by love for others,
then I am not truly one with Christ.
And if I truly know Christ,
then love will rule my life.

Beloved, let us love one another:
for love is of God; and every one
that loveth is born of God,
and knoweth God.
1 JOHN 4:7

I see one path which you have not tried,
which can lead you out of these sore straits.
You have tried living for yourself a good many years,
and the result is great weariness and heaviness of soul.
Try now to live for others.

The more Christlike I become,
the more I shall be filled
with love for every living thing.

It is easy to forgive when one loves.

My Fellow Travelers

We look at our fellowmen too much from the standpoint of our own prejudices. They may be wrong; they may have their faults and foibles; they may call out all the meanest and most hateful in us. But they are not all wrong; they have their virtues, and when they excite our bad passions by their own, they may be as ashamed and sorry as we are irritated. And I think some of the best, most contrite, most useful men and women, whose prayers prevail with God and bring down blessings into the homes in which they dwell, often possess unlovely traits that furnish them with their best discipline. The very fact that they are ashamed of themselves drives them to God; they feel safe in His presence. And while they lie in the very dust of self-confusion at His feet, they are dear to Him and have power with Him.

*F*our steps lead to peace:

- Be desirous of doing the will of another, rather than thine own.

- Choose always to have less, rather than more.

- Seek always the lowest place, and to be inferior to everyone.

- Wish always, and pray, that the will of God may be wholly fulfilled in thee.

from *The Imitation of Christ,*
by Thomas à Kempis, one of Katy's favorite authors.

If a man say, I love God, and hateth his brother, he is a liar:
for he that loveth not his brother whom he hath seen,
how can he love God whom he hath not seen?
1 JOHN 4:20

A Companion on the Road: Married Life

ociety tells me many fairy tales about married love–
and when the romance looks as though it has died,
I may be tempted to leave my marriage and look for yet another
fairy tale. The truth is, however, that married life requires prayer
if it is to last and grow–and only God can bring married love
to its deepest and truest fruition.

Nevertheless let every one of you in particular
so love his wife even as himself; and the wife
see that she reverence her husband.
EPHESIANS 5:33

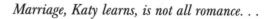

> *Our love has felt conscious of resting on a rock—and that rock was the will of God.*

Marriage, Katy learns, is not all romance. . .

We are imperfect creatures, wayward and foolish as little children, horribly unreasonable, selfish, and willful. We are not capable of enduring the shock of finding, at every turn, that our idol is made of clay and that it is prone to tumble off its pedestal and lie in the dust till we pick it up and set it in its place again. I was struck with my husband's asking in the very first prayer he offered in my presence, after our marriage, that God would help us love each other; I felt that love was the very foundation of which I was built and that there was no danger that I should ever fall short in giving my husband all he wanted in full measure. But as he went on day after day repeating this prayer, and I naturally made it with him, I came to see that this most precious of earthly blessings has been and must be God's gift, and that while we both looked at it in that light and felt our dependence on Him for it, we might safely encounter together all the assaults made upon us by the world, the flesh, and the devil.

Two are better than one. . . . For if they fall, the one
will lift up his fellow: but woe to him that is alone when he falleth;
for he hath not another to help him up.
Ecclesiastes 4:9–10

Happiness, in other words, love, in married life is not a mere accident.
When the union has been formed, as most Christian unions are,
by God Himself, it is His intention and His will that it shall prove
the unspeakable joy of both husband and wife and become
more and more so from year to year.

We have modified each other. My husband is more demonstrative,
more attentive to those little things that make the happiness
of married life; and I am less childish, less vehement.

Every day that a husband and wife walk hand in hand together upon this earth makes the twain more and more one flesh. The selfish element that at first formed so large a part of their attraction to each other disappears, and the union becomes so pure and beautiful as to form a fitting type of the union of Christ and His church. There is nothing else on earth like it.

Therefore shall a man leave his father and his mother, and shall cleave unto his wife: and they shall be one flesh.

GENESIS 2:24

God has blessed our married life; it has had its waves and billows, but, thanks be unto Him, it has settled down into a calm sea of untroubled peace.

Breaking the Path for Those Who Follow: Christian Motherhood

*B*eing a mother is an awesome responsibility. It requires spiritual discipline, self-sacrifice, and flexibility. But as a mother, I do not carry this responsibility alone, for God works with me, giving me His strength and compassion when I am weak and tired, blessing both my children and myself. Motherhood may be a demanding life, it is true—but it is also one of great delight, an opportunity to experience God's grace and joy.

*"And whoso shall receive
one such little child
in my name receiveth me."*
MATTHEW 18:5

I am so glad I was ever born into this beautiful world,
where there will always be dear little children to love!

The best convent for a woman is the seclusion of her own home.
There she may find her vocation and fight her battles,
and there she may learn the reality and the earnestness of life.

When you speak contemptuously of the vocation of maternity,
you dishonor not only the mother who bore you
but the Lord Jesus Himself, who chose to be born of woman
and to be ministered unto by her through a helpless infancy.

Breaking the Path for Those Who Follow

When Katy gives birth to her second child, she wonders,

Where does all the love come from? If I had had her always, I do not see how I could be more fond of her. And do people call it living who never had any children?

Katy struggles with her young children. . .

I find little Ernest has a passionate temper and a good deal of self-will. But he has fine qualities. I wish he had a better mother. I am so impatient with him when he is wayward and perverse! What he needs is a firm, gentle hand, moved by no caprice and controlled by the constant fear of God. . . . He never ought to hear an irritable word or a sharp tone; but he does hear them, I must own with grief and shame. . . . Next to being a perfect wife, I want to be a perfect mother. How mortifying, how dreadful in all things to come short of even one's own standard!

And all thy children shall be taught
of the LORD;
and great shall be the peace
of thy children.
Isaiah 54:13

*This world needs to be adorned
with lovely little ones.*

If He should take our baby away, I would still rejoice that this life was mingled with ours and has influenced us. Yes, even an unconscious infant is an ever-felt influence in the household. What an amazing thought!

I have given this precious little one away to her Savior and to mine; living or dying, she is His.

We will give our children to Him if He asks for them.
He will never have to snatch them away from us by force.

As a mother, Katy believes that children should be taught God's love rather than their own sinfulness. Katy's father-in-law, however, cannot understand Katy's joyful approach to faith. . .

"I hope, my daughter, that you are faithful to your son. I hope you teach him that he is a sinner and that he is in a state of condemnation."

"No, Father, I don't," I said. "You are all tired out and don't know what you are saying. I would not have little Ernest hear you for the world."

Poor Father! He fairly groaned. "You are responsible for the child's soul," he said. "You have more influence over him than all the world beside."

"I know it," I said, "and sometimes I feel ready to sink when I think of the great work God has entrusted to me. But my child will learn he is a sinner only too soon; I want to fortify his soul with the only antidote against the misery that knowledge will give him. I want him to see his Redeemer in all His love and all His beauty and to love Him with all his heart and soul and mind and strength."

Katy's sister-in-law is less than delighted when Katy gives birth to yet another child. . .

She says I shall now have one more mouth to fill and two feet the more to shoe, more disturbed nights, more laborious days, and less leisure or visiting, reading, music, and drawing.

Well! This is one side of the story, to be sure, but I look at the other. Here is a sweet, fragrant mouth to kiss; here are two more feet to make music pattering about my nursery. Here is a soul to train for God; and the body in which it dwells is worthy all it will cost, since it is the abode of a kingly tenant. I may see less of friends, but I have gained one more dearer than them all, to whom, while I minister in Christ's name, I make a willing sacrifice of what little leisure for my own recreation my other darlings had left me. Yes, my precious baby, you are welcome to your mother's heart, welcome to her time, her strength, her health, her tenderest cares, to her lifelong prayers! Oh, how rich I am, how truly, how wondrously blest!

Provoke not your children to wrath: but bring them up in the nurture and admonition of the Lord.
EPHESIANS 6:4

Jesus. . .said unto them, "Suffer the little children to come unto me,
and forbid them not: for of such is the kingdom of God."
Mark 10:14

I am only afraid it is only too true, as someone has remarked,
that "this is the age of obedient parents!" What then will be the future
of their children? How can they yield to God who have never been
taught to yield to human authority? And how well will they be fitted
to rule their own households who have never learned to rule themselves?

I have learned, at last, not to despise the day of small things,
to cherish the tenderest blossom, and to expect my dear ones
to be imperfect before they become perfect.

A disciplined mother—disciplined children.

Therefore shall ye lay up these my words in your heart
and in your soul. . . . And ye shall teach them your children,
speaking of them when thou sittest in thine house,
and when thou walkest by the way, when thou liest down,
and when thou risest up.
Deuteronomy 11:18–19

Breaking the Path for Those Who Follow

Oh! I am so selfish, and it is so hard to practice the very law of love I preach to my children! Yet I want this law to rule and reign in my home, that it may be a little heaven below; and I will not, no, I will not cease praying that it may be such, no matter what it costs me.

The coming of each new child strengthens and deepens my desire to be what I would have it become, makes my fault more odious in my eyes, and elevates my whole character. What a blessed discipline of joy and of pain my life has been; how thankful I am to reap its fruits even while pricked by its thorns!

I have often felt in moments of bitter grief at my impatience with my children that perhaps God pitied me more than He blamed me for it!

He shall. . .gently lead those that are with young.
Isaiah 40:11

*The best way to instruct children in faith,
is to link every little daily act of a child's life
with the Divine Love, that Divine Life
that gives meaning to all things.*

With my children I always aim for flexibility. I think a mother, especially, ought to learn to enter into the gayer moods of her children at the very moment when her own heart is sad. And it may be as religious an act for her to romp with them at one time as to pray with them at another.

An Ordinary Journey: Finding God in Everyday Life

I tend to think of serving God in terms of grand, heroic acts—but serving Him daily, in all the everyday and trivial events of my life, actually requires far more discipline and commitment. Something as ordinary as doing the laundry or cleaning a bathroom can lead my heart to God, so long as I offer everything I do up to Him.

Then said Jesus unto his disciples,
"If any man will come after me,
let him deny himself,
and take up his cross,
and follow me."
MATTHEW 16:24

An Ordinary Journey

Content yourself for the present with doing in a faithful, quiet,
persistent way all the little, homely tasks that return with each returning
day, each one as unto God, and perhaps by and by you
will thus have gained strength for a more heroic life.

You may depend upon it that a life of real heroism and self-sacrifice
must begin and lay its foundation in this little world wherein
it learns its first lesson and takes its first steps.

God notices the most trivial act, accepts the poorest, most threadbare
little service, listens to the coldest, feeblest petition, and gathers up
with parental fondness all our fragmentary desires and attempts at
good works. Oh, if we could only begin to conceive how
He loves us, what different creatures we should be!

"And whosoever shall give to drink unto one of these little ones a cup
of cold water only in the name of a disciple, verily I say unto you,
he shall in no wise lose his reward."
Matthew 10:42

*Duty looks more repelling at a distance
than when fairly faced and met.*

As you penetrate the labyrinth of life in pursuit of Christian duty,
you will often be surprised and charmed by meeting your Master
Himself amid its windings and turnings and receive
His soul-inspiring smile. You will always meet Him,
wherever you go.

An Ordinary Journey

It sweetens every bit of work to think that I am doing it in humble,
far-off, yet real imitation of Jesus.

"Verily I say unto you, Inasmuch as ye have done it unto one
of the least of these my brethren, ye have done it unto me."
Matthew 25:40

Mrs. Campbell gives Katy good advice on keeping our love for
God and our love for our families in proper perspective:

"You think then," I said while my heart died within me, "that husband
and children are obstacles in our way and hinder our getting near to Christ?"

"Oh, no!" she cried. "God never gives us hindrances. On the contrary,
He means, in making us wives and mothers, to put us into the very conditions of holy living."

*"If any man serve me,
let him follow me;
and where I am, there
shall also my servant be:
if any man serve me, him
will my Father honour."*
JOHN 12:26

How can one help but carry religion into everything,
if one's religion is a vital part of one's self, not a cloak put on
to go to church in and hang up out of the way
against next Sunday?

Katy learns much from the writings of Fenelon:

QUESTION: How shall I offer my purely indifferent actions to God; walks, visits made and received, dress, other amusements, such as shopping, having clothes made, and equipages? I want to have some sort of prayer method of offering each of these things to God.

REPLY: The most indifferent actions cease to be such and become good as soon as one performs them with the intention of conforming one's self to the will of God. They are often better and purer than certain actions that appear more virtuous. These little occasions occur more frequently and furnish a secret occasion for continually making every moment profitable.

It is not necessary to make great efforts nor acts of great reflection in order to offer what are called indifferent actions. It is enough to lift the soul one instant to God, to make a simple offering of it. Everything which God wishes us to do, and which enters into the course of occupation suitable to our position, can and ought to be offered to God; nothing is unworthy of Him but sin.

One must take life as it comes; its homely details are so mixed up with its sweet charities and loves and friendships that one is forced to believe that God joined them together and does not will that they should be put asunder.

The top of the ladder that rests on earth reaches to heaven, and we may ascend it as the angels did in Jacob's dream.

What a blessed life that must be, when the base things of this world and things that are despised are so many links to the invisible world and to the things God has chosen.

> *"He that is faithful in that which is least is faithful also in much: and he that is unjust in the least is unjust also in much."*
>
> <small>LUKE 16:10</small>

Instead of fancying that our ordinary daily work was one thing and our religion quite another thing, we should transmute our drudgery into acts of worship. Instead of going to prayer meetings to get into a "good frame," we should live in a good frame from morning till night, from night till morning; and prayer and praise would be only another form for expressing the love and faith and obedience we had been exercising amid the pressure of business.

I have made prayer too much of a luxury and have often inwardly chafed and fretted when the care of my children, at times, made it utterly impossible to leave them for private devotion—when they have been sick, for instance, or other like emergencies. I reasoned this way: "Here is a special demand on my patience, and I am naturally impatient. I must have time to go away and entreat the Lord to equip me for this conflict." But I see now that the simple act of cheerful acceptance of the duty imposed and the solace and support withdrawn would have united me more fully to Christ than the highest enjoyment of His presence in prayer could.

How little they know who languish in what seem useless sickrooms or amid the restrictions of frail health, what work they do for Christ by the power of saintly living and by even fragmentary prayers.

Traveling Faster:
Becoming Who God Wants Me to Be

God does not call me to fit a certain mold, nor does He want to press out of bunch of cookie-cutter Christians, each one exactly alike. No, when God created me, He made me a unique individual with particular gifts and abilities. This is my true self, and as I become this person that God intended, I find that I am happier and more free. I am also more united with the Holy Spirit, able to take the place God calls me to in His kingdom.

I will praise thee;
for I am fearfully and wonderfully made:
marvellous are thy works;
and that my soul knoweth right well.
PSALM 139:14

Speaking beautifully is little to the purpose unless
one lives beautifully.

*You may depend upon it that people
are as individual in their piety as in other things
and cannot all be shaped in one mold.*

I have a great many little trials, but they don't do me a bit of good. Or, at least, I don't see that they do."

"No, we never see plants growing," Mrs. Campbell answered.

"And do you really think, then, that perhaps I am growing, though unconsciously?"

"I know you are, dear child. There can't be life without growing."

Thou hast planted them, yea,
     they have taken root:
they grow, yea, they bring forth fruit.
     Jeremiah 12:2

I see that the Christian life
must be individual,
as the natural character is, and
that I cannot be exactly
like any other saint, though
they all stimulate
and are an inspiration to me.

My very best is my real self.

*We learn as fast
as we are willing to learn.
God does not force
instruction upon us,
but when we say
as Luther did,
"More light, Lord, more light,"
the light comes.*

Thy word is a lamp unto my feet,
and a light unto my path.
Psalm 119:105

There is no use in trying to engraft an opposite nature
on one's own. What I am, that I must be, except
as God changes me into His own image.
And everything brings me back to that,
as my supreme desire.

*Why should the children of the King
go mourning all their days?*

I see more and more that I must be myself what I want my children
to be and that I cannot make myself over even for their sakes.
This must be His work.

Journey's End: Reaching Heaven

*M*other keeps saying I spend too much time in brooding over my sorrows. As for her, she seems to live in heaven. Not that she has long prosy talks about it, but little words that she lets drop now and then show where her thoughts are and where she would like to be. She seems to think everybody is as eager to go there as she is. For my part, I am not eager at all. I can't make myself feel that it will be nice to sit in rows, all the time singing, fond as I am of music. And when I say to myself, "Of course we shall not always sit in rows singing," then I fancy a multitude of shadowy, phantomlike beings, dressed in white, moving to and fro in golden streets, doing nothing in particular, and having a dreary time, without anything to look forward to.

I told Mother so. She said earnestly and yet in her sweetest, tenderest way, "Oh, my darling Katy! What you need is such a living, personal love of Christ to make the thought of being where He is so delightful as to fill your mind with the single thought."

Journey's End

The world I live in tells me that death is something to be feared.
If I truly believe the gospel, though, death is only coming home at last,
to my true home in heaven.

And God shall wipe away all tears from their eyes; and there
shall be no more death, neither sorrow, nor crying, neither shall
there be any more pain: for the former things are passed away.
REVELATION 21:4

So when this corruptible shall have put on incorruption,
and this mortal shall have put on immortality, then shall be brought
to pass the saying that is written, Death is swallowed up in victory.
O death, where is thy sting? O grave, where is thy victory?
1 Corinthians 15:54–55

Caroline Fry's confidence lasted until the day of her death,
when she expressed these thoughts:

This is my bridal-day, the beginning of my life.
I wish there should be no mistake about
the reason of my desire to depart and be with Christ.
I desire to go to Him that I may be rid of the burden of sin.

*"Rejoice, and be exceeding glad:
for great is your reward in heaven."*
MATTHEW 5:12

Track	Title	Time	© ℗
1	O My God You Are So Glorious	2:41	(2)
2	Father I Need	3:35	(2)
3	Jesus, You Are the Radiance	3:24	(1)
4	How Majestic Is Your Name	3:12	(2)
5	Give Me a Heart	2:46	(2)
6	Be Free	3:08	(1)
7	I Lift Up My Hands/ I Will Serve No Foreign God	5:23	(1)
8	Send Your Spirit	2:52	(2)
9	Show Me Your Way O Lord	2:38	(2)
10	I Just Want to Praise You	2:44	(1)

TOTAL RUNNING TIME (32:29)